D1714143

The Book of
LANDRY

The Book of
LANDRY

Words of Wisdom from and
Testimonials to TOM LANDRY,
Former Coach of America's Team

Compiled by
Jennifer Briggs Kaski

TowleHouse Publishing Company
Nashville, Tennessee

Distributed to the trade by Cumberland House Publishing, 431 Harding Industrial Drive, Nashville, Tennessee 37211.

This is a work that has not been authorized by Tom Landry or his estate. It includes quotes about and by Tom Landry compiled by the author through firsthand interviews as well as from research of previously published material.

A portion of the royalties from the sale of this book will be donated to the Fellowship of Christian Athletes.

Cataloging-in-Publication data is available.
ISBN: 0-9668774-3-8

Page design by Mike Towle

Printed in the United States of America

1 2 3 4 5 6 — 04 03 02 01 00

To Hershizer,
because the Lord blesses us
in profound ways

Contents

Preface

February 16, 2000, was an unusually warm winter day. The men Tom Landry carried to Super Bowls and playoff games—Waters, Lilly, White, Dorsett, Pearson—carried him to his grave. In suits and ties they cried, much like Landry cried before his players the day he had to leave the Cowboys. Out of nowhere, a flock of F-16s boomed across the sky above the deceased war hero.

It was his last surprise play, some said that day. They pulled a burial off with four hundred in attendance, and, in perhaps the greatest tribute to the respect they had for his memory, every single one kept the secret. Guys like Hollywood Henderson, who caused a world of trouble with the Cowboys, roamed the cemetery for what seemed like an hour after the burial.

"I guess I'm like the wayward child who finally appreciates his father after he's gone," Henderson said.

The next day, a memorial service was held for the family and for the public. Even media people couldn't keep it together. Flags flew halfway down poles, and tears rolled down grown people's cheeks. Men wiped eyes with fingers bearing Super Bowl rings and walked away from interviews they just couldn't finish.

Roger Staubach read from Corinthians.

Henderson, whom Landry basically fired, wept into his hand, "I never knew a better man than Tom Landry."

Day in, day out, for seventy-five years and twenty-nine seasons, few could have.

8

Introduction

SOMETIMES IT is almost tough to think of him as a go-getter. Tony Dorsett wondered how a guy could never yell. Just any guy.

Others wonder how a guy who never yelled, could coach.

But Tom Landry isn't just any guy.

He coached the Dallas Cowboys for twenty-nine years and ranks as the third-winningest coach in National Football League history, behind George Halas and Don Shula. Then there were the eighteen play-off appearances and five Super Bowls.

Landry had a way—a weird way in the minds of the players, but it worked. They look back and describe it as genius.

It does seem like a stretch, this painfully shy child from Mission, Texas, with a speech impediment and a Texas drawl, rising to such a state of brilliance.

"Genius," the former players call it over and over.

HIS EARLY summers as an assistant coach in New York were marked with frugality. He had to work summers to provide for wife, Alicia, and eventually their three children.

So, he sold insurance, in New York of all places, with a lisp and a drawl, and he ended up in the million-dollar roundtable. He finished his industrial engineering degree in the off-seasons as well.

"That says something," says Bob Lilly.

That says a lot more than most of us ever heard Tom say about anything but football.

He was born among the dirt and palm trees of Mission, Texas, on September 11, 1924. They say the boy named best-looking his senior year never asked a girl to dance in high school.

The Fireman's Park in Mission is named for his dad, Ray, a Sunday school teacher with an auto repair shop.

His mom was Ruth, and he is the middle child of three.

There was no predicting what would come.

A few years ago, Tom Landry said he and his friend Vince Lombardi were really very much alike.

Now that I have done similar books on Lombardi and Landry, I see what Coach means.

"Well," said Dan Reeves, the Atlanta Falcons' coach, considering the comparison, "you know, come to think of it, they are a lot alike."

Lombardi's compassion and his passion were outward. Landry is a flat-out introvert. Those close to him, including his pastor who has corralled him into many church speeches, say he hates that public-speaking stuff.

Hates it? The man who has stood before Billy Graham Crusades and spoken at length about his faith? The man who sang in a commercial? The Christian role model who has made hundreds of appearances at FCA banquets?

There are no pat answers as to why Tom Landry is so revered by so many. Yet he is almost intimidating to talk to at times—though he really doesn't mean to come off that way.

I DON'T KNOW how many times I've interviewed him,
but every time I do, I'm a little nervous.

Why would I talk to President George Bush like
we're about to go bass fishing together, but when I
call Tom Landry on the phone or trap him on a golf
course at a post-firing training camp, I get the feeling
I won't be this nervous when I talk to God himself
someday and He tells me everything I did wrong that
I already knew and even the stuff I didn't know was
wrong and did?

I just really don't have a good answer. The other
people who have known him don't really know either.

But they've done their best, capturing the persona
of this genuine, caring, compassionate man, a man of
more patience than any toddler's mother or, well, football coach.

Yeah, they probably tell it best, the story of this
enigmatic man, as deceptive as his flex defense—it
really wasn't as hard to figure out as people thought, it
just looked that way.

Yes, Coach was a lot like his plays—more intimidating in appearance than in up-close interaction.

And that is why he won.

THERE WERE other parts of Landry.

I learned about faith from my father. He went to church, read his Bible every night.

He was basically quiet. He didn't smile a lot but his smile had this unmistakable thing about it. I think it's called the peace that passes all understanding. And if you saw "the Look," it was just like the eye dagger Landry put through men's hearts without saying a single word.

Daddy was a big Landry fan, and I learned from him about football and Landry. It was my father's personality that helped me understand and revere Landry as a father figure very early in life.

Landry was a second reinforcement that there were good people out there who didn't say much more than an occasional *hell* and *damn*, didn't watch dirty movies or even TV that wasn't wholesome—and that was in the late sixties and seventies. People such as Landry and my dad create a standard of conduct we should aspire to. They tell us that others should be that way as well, and we are entitled to the respect that comes to us when those around us observe such a code of ethics.

But I never understood the man, really, until this project was near completion.

Shy, not cold. Objective, not aloof. Spiritually patient, not pushy. And the list goes on.

Landry taught us long ago that there are standards out there that are worth asking for in our friends and spouses, and worth striving for as individuals. Not everyone is cut out to be a Landry. Such greatness is born of odd combinations—the shyness juxtaposed with smarts. Smarts combined with a rigid work ethic. A teacher or coach who impacts us at just the right time, as Landry's high school coach did.

Others tell it best.

—Jennifer Briggs Kaski
January 2000

The Book of
LANDRY

1

Landry and His Youth

~

 THE OLDER ladies in Mission, Texas, remember him as mommas would—a very "clean" boy.

He spent most of his time playing pickup football. The "flex" may have germinated on an empty lot of sand and broken glass in this once-small town, where Landry was a high school football star too shy to ask a girl to dance.

After the war, where he saw places so much more diverse than Texas Valley, Tommy Landry blossomed as he entered the University of Texas and discovered dating and other enjoyableactivities.

His mother and my mother were always together. We'd
gone down to McAllen with our mothers to buy shoes.
He was always doing something he wasn't supposed to
do, and he didn't mind. His mother was always asking
him to mind and that time he didn't, and he fell out of
the car and broke his arm.

—Marvel Rhodes, cousin

He was very quiet and conservative. I wouldn't say he
was a loaner, but . . .

—Eddie Hedges, childhood friend

**Fact: Tom Landry, voted Mission High School's
Cutest Boy, was too shy to ask a girl to dance
until after he had fought in a war and become a
football star at the University of Texas.**

You know he was just a young man. Very clean.
—*Dorothy Hedges*, *childhood friend*

He loved (comic) funny books. And he didn't want me reading his funny books. "Leave 'em alone." He'd study those funny books.

Even when he was little he was always playing football and thinking about football in the sandlot.
—*Marvel Rhodes*

I thought he'd be an average man. I didn't think he'd go on to what he became. There was no way you could see any future greatness in him. Hell, he was just like the rest of us, just an ordinary kid.
—*Jimmy Mehis*, *childhood friend*

Humility was, and remains, a Landry trademark. One recollection of youthful misfortune in his boyhood home of Mission, Texas, explains why:

BUT ONE DAY I EITHER PEDALED TOO FAST, HIT A PARTICULARLY BAD RUT, OR SIMPLY PANICKED—MAYBE ALL THREE. WHATEVER THE CAUSE, I CRASHED INTO THE ROAD BANK SO HARD I FLEW HEAD OVER HANDLEBARS AND LANDED ON MY BOTTOM, SMACK IN THE MIDDLE OF A LARGE CLUSTER OF CACTUS.

I JUMPED UP AND LIT OUT FOR HOME SCREAMING FOR MAMA. BUT THE PAIN IN MY POSTERIOR WAS NOTHING COMPARED TO THE EMBARRASSMENT I SUFFERED OVER HER QUICK-THINKING SOLUTION TO MY PRICKLY PREDICAMENT. SOMEHOW SHE SENT OUT THE ALARM . . . AND THE NEXT THING I KNEW I WAS LYING FACE DOWN AND BARE-BOTTOM UP ON A TABLE SURROUNDED BY NEIGHBOR LADIES ARMED WITH TWEEZERS.

I HAVE NO IDEA HOW LONG IT TOOK, BUT IT SEEMED LIKE HOURS AS MY MOTHER AND HER FRIENDS PULLED SCORES OF NEEDLES FROM MY BACKSIDE.[1]

—Landry

ONE OF MY EARLIEST MEMORIES IS FISHING WITH GRANDPA LANDRY AND MY DAD'S BROTHER, UNCLE ARTHUR. WE'D SPENT A LAZY AFTERNOON FISHING THE RIO GRANDE WHERE THE OLD PUMP STATION DIVERTED RIVER WATER INTO THE CANAL THAT SUPPLIED MISSION AND THE LOCAL CITRUS GROVES. WE'D CAUGHT THREE CATFISH BEFORE UNCLE ARTHUR ANNOUNCED, "IT'S TIME TO GO BACK HOME, TOMMY. YOU CAN BRING THE FISH."

I HAULED THE STRINGER OF FISH OUT OF THE WATER AND HEADED ACROSS THE CATWALK STRETCHING ACROSS THE CANAL. BUT MY BARE FEET SLIPPED ON THE WET, WOODEN WALKWAY AND I PLUNGED INTO THE WATER CHURNING OUT FROM UNDER THE PUMP HOUSE. NO SOONER DID THAT DARK BROWN WATER CLOSE OVER MY HEAD THAT I FELT A BIG ADULT HAND GRAB MY HAIR AND DRAG ME BACK UP INTO THE LIGHT. ONE MOMENT OF TERRIFYING DARKNESS WAS ALL I FELT BEFORE UNCLE ARTHUR WAS THERE. AND WHEN HE PULLED ME SAFELY OUT OF THAT RUSHING WATER, HE AND GRANDPA EXCLAIMED IN AMAZEMENT, "WOULD YOU LOOK AT THAT! TOMMY NEVER LET GO OF THE FISH!" THERE THEY WERE! I HAD THE STRINGER OF CATFISH STILL TIGHTLY CLENCHED IN MY HAND.[2]

—*Landry*

Tommy was the leader, even then, before we even got into high school. We'd choose up sides. A kid might be too little or just not very good, and nobody would pick him for their side. A lot of guys would tell the kid to go, just leave us alone. Not Tommy. I can remember he'd say, "Let him play on my side." Then he'd take the kid aside and say, "You can play. You can do it. Don't let them tell you any different. You can always play on my team."[3]

—*Joe Summers, childhood friend*

THERE WASN'T MUCH IN THE WAY OF ORGANIZED ACTIVITIES IN MISSION, BUT THEN WE DIDN'T NEED ANY. MY FRIENDS AND I PLAYED FOOTBALL AND BASKETBALL IN SEASON—SOMETIMES DOWN AT THE PARK, BUT MORE OFTEN IN OUR YARD OR IN THE VACANT LOT NEXT TO OUR HOUSE. WE LIVED OUTDOORS AND WENT BAREFOOT PRETTY MUCH YEAR-ROUND; I DON'T REMEMBER REGULARLY WEARING SHOES UNTIL JUNIOR HIGH. . . . I LEARNED TO SWIM IN THE IRRIGATION CANALS OUTSIDE TOWN. . . . WE WOULD HIKE DOWN TO THE RIO GRANDE TO FISH WHENEVER WE WANTED, AND COME HUNTING SEASON, WE'D TAKE TO THE FIELDS OUTSIDE TOWN TO HUNT DEER AND SHOOT WHITE-WING DOVES THAT FLEW IN FLOCKS SO BIG THEY SOMETIMES DARKENED THE SKY.[4]

—*Landry*

UNLIKE KIDS TODAY WHO OFTEN IDOLIZE BIG-NAME ATHLETES, I KNEW LITTLE OR NOTHING ABOUT ORGANIZED PROFESSIONAL SPORTS. ONCE IN A WHILE I'D SIT WITH THE OLD BLACK GENTLE-MAN WHO SHINED SHOES AT THE BARBER SHOP AND LISTEN TO A BROADCAST OF A NEW YORK YANKEES GAME. EVEN IN MISSION WE KNEW ABOUT THE YANKEES. BUT I COULDN'T HAVE NAMED A HALF-DOZEN BIG-LEAGUE BASEBALL TEAMS. AND I NEVER KNEW THERE WAS SUCH A THING AS PROFESSIONAL FOOTBALL.

SO I DIDN'T FIND MY BOYHOOD HEROES ON THE PLAYING FIELD. I WATCHED THEM IN WESTERN MOVIES, RIDING ACROSS FIELDS ON HORSEBACK. WHENEVER I IMAGINED A GLAMOROUS AND EXCITING FUTURE LIFE BEYOND THE BORDERS OF MISSION, TEXAS, I ALWAYS DREAMED OF BECOMING A COWBOY.[5]

—Landry

MY FAMILY, MY CHURCH, AND THE SMALL-TOWN ENVIRONMENT OF MISSION SERVED AS THE FILTERS FOR THE BASIC VALUES I LEARNED AS A BOY. BUT IT WAS SPORTS THAT SHAPED AND REINFORCED THOSE VALUES.[6]

—Landry

He never had to fight. He never rubbed anybody wrong and even the bullies wouldn't pick on him. He was a pretty good-sized kid and could be very . . . well, firm.[7]

—Joe Summers, childhood friend

ABOUT TWO DOZEN BOYS TURNED OUT FOR THE FIRST DAY OF JUNIOR VARSITY PRACTICE. WHEN COACH (BOB) MARTIN HELD UP A FOOTBALL AND SAID, "I NEED A SMART, TOUGH KID WHO WILL TAKE THIS BALL AND INITIATE EVERY PLAY FOR OUR TEAM," I IMMEDIATELY VOLUNTEERED. I BELIEVED I WAS TOUGH, BUT I'M NOT SURE HOW SMART I WAS BECAUSE THAT'S HOW I BECAME THE 112-POUND CENTER OF THE MISSION HIGH SCHOOL JUNIOR VARSITY FOOTBALL TEAM. I'D RATHER HAVE BEEN A BACK, BUT MY JV EXPERIENCE AS A CENTER HELPED TEACH ME THE IMPORTANCE OF TEAMWORK.[8]

—Landry

Landry, recalling the "single most influential person in his life," Mission High football coach Bob Martin:

HE CONVINCED ME THAT SUCCESS ALWAYS REQUIRES EFFORT. THAT SELF-RESPECT DEMANDS YOUR MAXIMUM EFFORT AT ALL TIMES. AND THAT YOUR BEST EFFORT ALWAYS MADE YOU A WINNER BECAUSE IT MEANT YOU'D NEVER LOSE YOUR PRIDE . . . HE MODELED SELF-DISCI-PLINE IN HIS OWN LIFE AND DEMANDED NO LESS FROM HIS ATHLETES. AND I LISTENED BECAUSE I KNEW WHAT BOB MARTIN SAID, HE ALSO LIVED . . . HIS WORD WOULD BECOME MY LAW, HIS APPROVAL MY INSPIRA-TION. AND FOOTBALL WOULD BECOME MY LIFE.[9]

—Landry

One weekend when Landry's mom visited him (at UT), she was riding in the front seat of his car while two teammates rode in the back. She happened to pull down the sun visor and a pair of panties fell in her lap.

"What's this?" she asked her son.

"Oh," Landry said, "those are from my score last night." Tom wasn't Mr. Perfect. No. He was just like a lot of college guys.[10]

At age twenty-four, Tom Landry was a strapping six-foot-one, 185-pound back for the Texas Longhorns. (AP/Wide World Photos)

We knew he was a class guy. He was a big, raw-boned kid—and a tremendous punter, too. He could turn and back-pedal and seemed a natural on defense. He had a lot of courage and would really come up and bust the ballcarrier.

I can remember when we first began checking up on him. I talked to Dutch Meyer at TCU and he said, "He's a hoss. Landry's a hoss."[11]

—Jack White, assistant coach for the professional football Yankees, recalling his teams scouting report on UT senior fullback Tom Landry

2

Landry and Humor

PLAYERS RECALL two times they played jokes on Landry. Due to his focused nature, the ploys went right over his head, as humor sometimes did. One time at Thousand Oaks, quarterback Don Meredith got one of his stuntmen pals to apply a large, bloody gash to the football star's face. That's how Meredith looked as he arrived at the team dinner. A few guys said they thought Coach was going to pass out.

Another time, Walt Garrison, wearing a gruesome mask some described as Herman Munster-like and wearing old, dirty clothes, brought in Tom's birthday cake at the coach's birthday party.

"That might be the most startled I ever saw him," said Lee Roy Jordan.

Landry was no normal guy. He had a great capacity to love, but didn't exactly show it.

He was intelligent in many areas, but really only used the big smarts on football.

Those interviewed mostly recalled that he could be funny, but a lot of stuff just went over his hat.

Usually, however, he was clever by accident.

It was that quality, combined with his dry Texas humor he usually kept buried, that actually made him kind of funny sometimes—not much, but sometimes.

Always, his humor was innocent.

He's pretty clever sometimes, but I don't think he does it on purpose.

—*Walt Garrison*

He didn't have a sense of humor while I was playing, but after he retired we saw a difference.

—*Chuck Howley*

Tom had a sense of humor. He just didn't get it that well. He was humorous at times, but . . .

—*Lee Roy Jordan*

In a personality contest between Tom Landry and Bud Grant, there would be no winner.[1]
—*Don Meredith, in quip spoken during an* ABC Monday Night Football *meeting between the Cowboys and Minnesota Vikings (whose Hall-of-Fame coach was equally stoic on the sidelines)*

I WALKED OVER TO CHECK ON ROGER [STAUBACH] AND HIS
BLEEDING LIP. "YOU KNOW, ROGER," I SAID, TRYING NOT TO
SMILE, "FOR A WHILE, EVERY TIME YOU LOOK IN THE MIRROR TO
SHAVE YOU'RE GONNA HAVE A REMINDER NOT TO CHANGE MY
PLAYS." BUT ROGER GOT HIS DIGS IN, TOO. ONE DAY AS HE CAME
OFF THE FIELD AFTER THROWING AN INTERCEPTION, I MET HIM
AT THE SIDELINES ASKING, "WHY DID YOU THROW THAT PASS?
THE DEFENSIVE MAN HAD HIM COVERED." ROGER SNAPPED RIGHT
BACK, "WHY DID YOU CALL SUCH A RIDICULOUS PLAY?"[2]

—Landry

Landry's offense could make a rookie look like a
baboon with a reading disorder.

—Walt Garrison

This one particular day, a grain truck overturned on the
expressway about two miles north of the hotel and tied
traffic up forever. Four or five players got to the meeting about twenty minutes late. And so did Jim Myers,
the Cowboys' assistant head coach. Well, Jim is real
tight with a dollar, and the fine was $150 and that
included coaches. "Hey . . . a grain truck overturned,"

Jim said. "You shouldn't fine these guys. Or me." And Tom said, "You gotta plan for that. Plan for flat tires. Plan for congestion." That was it. Period.

In the nine years I played, I never saw Landry late for a meeting or anything else. Never. Now, you know over a nine-year period, something had to have gone wrong. So that meant he even planned for disaster.

—*Walt Garrison*

After the game was over, Landry was asked, "Tom, you heard about the bomb threat in the press box. What would you have done if all the writers had been blown up during the game?"

Landry thought for a second and without any expression on his stony face, took a deep breath and said, "Hmmm. I suppose we would have observed thirty seconds of silent prayer and then continued to play with all enthusiasm and vigor." Finally, he grinned again.[3]

—*Bob St. John, recalling a 1970 Cowboys game at old Yankee Stadium*

Sometimes stuff just went over his head. One time Tom got up and gave us this big talk about how he always coached better when he had oatmeal as his pregame meal. We were in New York, and one of the trainers starts the morning roll call. You've got to stand up and make your presence known and tell them what you want for breakfast.

"Adderly!"

"Oatmeal."

"Andrie!"

"Oatmeal."

"Bruenig!"

"Oatmeal."

"Cole!"

"Oatmeal."

Everybody ordered oatmeal and Tom didn't even flinch. He never realized it was a joke. We all had to go up to the trainer afterwards and tell him to cancel the forty orders of mush. Who could face the New York Giants on a bowl of oatmeal?

—*Walt Garrison*

When President Ford came to Dallas during the '76 election campaign, I invited him to visit Cowboys' headquarters. We arrived just before a scheduled quarterback strategy session, so I left the president in the hall and hurried into the meeting with Roger Staubach and Danny White.

"Fellas," I told them, "we've just picked up another quarterback for the Cowboys and I'd like you to meet him."

Danny and Roger got these uncertain expressions as I walked to the door. When I opened it, there stood the president of the United States with a big grin on his face and holding a football. My quarterbacks almost fell out of their chairs. Roger, old navy man that he was, looked as if he didn't know whether to shake his hand or salute.[4]

—Landry

Every play was a surprise. Confusion reigned like [droppings] at a horse show.

—Walt Garrison

Remembering his growing affection for Landry's early losing Cowboys teams, longtime Dallas newspaper sports columnist Blackie Sherrod says:

Damned right (we were beginning to like them). I mean, it was a terrible team, but it was our terrible team, you see?[5]

~

Donny Anderson was a rookie with the Packers when I was a rookie with the Cowboys. We played in the College All-Star Game together and we were friends. So we were talking one time before a game and Donny said, "Hell, this is just like playing at Texas Tech—cut-and-dried offense." Lombardi ran a straight-ahead offense. Green Bay would sweep to the right, then sweep left. Then on third down, they'd pass.

I told him about Landry's system and he said, "Holy [cow], Walt, how do you learn all that stuff?" And I answered, "I don't, Donny, I don't."

—*Walt Garrison*

~

Tom Landry was a one of a kind, all right. But he was just a coach, too. A great coach? Absolutely. But just a coach, a guy who made mistakes, who did the wrong thing sometimes . . . but probably a lot less than I have . . . and a man I was proud to know.[6]

—*Blackie Sherrod*

This is Landry in the 1950s as defensive backfield coach of the New York Giants. Among the players getting an earful are stars Sam Huff, kneeling, second from left; and Emlen Tunnell, standing in the middle in an unmarked sweatshirt. (AP/Wide World Photos)

3

Landry and Family

~

THE GRANDKIDS call him "Coach" now and then. Some players called him a nerd, because one of the NFL's best coaches preferred, in some respects, being called "Coach" by his grandkids than by his players.

Family has been first for Landry—before football and after God, ever since he became a Christian in 1959. He has one son, Tom Jr., and a daughter, Kitty. Another daughter, Lisa, recently died of cancer. Before the kids, there was always Alicia. You could call him *smitten*, a nice old-fashioned word Landry might use. Yes, smitten from the beginning to now.

Landry worked long hours but somehow found a balance others lose, that precarious scale weighing family and football films.

So, he'd just watch 'em at home. Ever supportive, Alicia said she didn't mind.

He still found time to read Golden Books to grandkids Jennifer and Ryan, and maybe a book or two about football.

ALICIA DIDN'T LIKE THE IDEA (OF A BLIND DATE), BUT GLORIA KEPT AFTER HER AND FINALLY PULLED RANK AS AN OLDER SORORITY SISTER—INSISTING THAT AS A PLEDGE, ALICIA HAD TO GO. SO WE WENT ON OUR FIRST DATE—A PICNIC IN THE WOODS AT BULL CREEK—THE DAY AFTER THE NORTH CAROLINA GAME. I MUST HAVE MADE QUITE AN IMPRESSION WHEN I SHOWED UP WITH MY BANDAGED THUMB, A SCRAPED-UP FACE, AND A BLACK EYE. I GUESS SHE TOOK PITY ON ME BECAUSE WE SEEMED TO HIT IT OFF.

NOT ONLY WAS SHE GOOD-LOOKING, BUT I FOUND HER EASY TO TALK TO AND FUN TO BE WITH. SO I ASKED HER OUT AGAIN THE NEXT WEEK. AND THE NEXT AND THE NEXT.[1]

—Landry

Landry recalls missing his then-pregnant new bride, Alicia, during his first professional football season (1949) with the New York Yankees Football Club of the short-lived All-American Football Conference:

DESPITE THE SHORTAGE OF PLAYING TIME, THE SEASON OFFERED A MEMORABLE INITIATION INTO PROFESSIONAL FOOTBALL LIFE. EVERY TRIP BECAME A PERSONAL FIRST—AN OPPORTUNITY FOR A COUNTRY BOY TO SEE YET ANOTHER BIG, INTERESTING AMERICAN CITY . . .

I LIVED DURING THE SEASON WITH A BUNCH OF OTHER SINGLE PLAYERS IN MANHATTAN AT THE OLD HENRY HUDSON HOTEL ON WEST FIFTY-SEVENTH. I WOULD CATCH THE SUBWAY UP TO YANKEE STADIUM FOR PRACTICE AND IN THE EVENINGS I'D GO OUT TO A MOVIE OR OVER TO MADISON SQUARE GARDEN TO WATCH A FIGHT. WHILE I ENJOYED EXPLORING THE BIG CITY, I VERY QUICKLY DEVELOPED A HORRIBLE CASE OF LONELINESS. I MISSED ALICIA SO MUCH I WROTE HER EVERY DAY AND COULD HARDLY WAIT UNTIL OUR GAME WAS OVER TO MAKE MY WEEKLY PHONE CALL HOME. THE CLOSER THE TIME TO THE BABY'S DUE DATE, THE MORE I WISHED I COULD JUST PACK UP AND HEAD HOME.[2]

—*Landry*

Landry's letter to his wife on the birth of his first child, Thomas Wade Landry Jr. . . .

MY DARLING WIFE,

WHEN I HEARD YOUR VOICE ON THE PHONE TONIGHT . . . I COULDN'T BELIEVE WE HAD A SON. I MUST HAVE SOUNDED ALL JUMBLED UP, BECAUSE I WANTED TO TELL YOU HOW GRAND IT WAS AND HOW MUCH I MISSED NOT BEING THERE, BUT ALL I SEEMED TO BE ABLE TO DO IS MUMBLE . . .

HAVE I TOLD YOU HOW MUCH I LOVE YOU? I WOULD LIKE TO TELL YOU A MILLION TIMES MORE THAT I DO. I GUESS TODAY I MISS YOU MORE THAN EVER. TO THINK TODAY WE HAVE BECOME THREE IS REALLY SOMETHING. I COULD ALMOST GET SENTIMENTAL, BUT YOU WOULD NEVER BELIEVE IT

. . . LET'S MAKE THIS NEXT MONTH FLY BY.

I LOVE YOU LOTS,

TOMMY, SR.[3]

It is February 1964, and Landry is all smiles after signing a new ten-year contract to remain as Dallas Cowboys head coach. Landry is flanked by Cowboys owner Clint Murchison Jr. (on left) and general manager Tex Schramm. (AP/Wide World Photos)

I'M NOT SURE MY FAMILY REALLY MINDED MISSING THE '74 PLAY-OFFS. WE WERE FINALLY ABLE TO USE THE CHRISTMAS HOLIDAYS FOR FAMILY TIME. WE EACH SELECTED JUST ONE OF THE PACKAGES UNDER OUR TREE TO OPEN ON A CHRISTMAS WEEK SKI TRIP TO CRESTED BUTTE, COLORADO. WE ALL LEARNED TO SKI, WENT CAROLING IN THE SNOW ON CHRISTMAS EVE, AND ENJOYED ONE OF OUR MOST MEMORABLE HOLIDAY SEASONS EVER.[4]

—Landry

When reminded that (Howard) Cosell, a strong Lombardi and Don Shula apostle, had been critical of Landry on *Monday Night Football*, often saying his team was over-rated, Landry just smiled and said nothing.

"Oh," said (his wife) Alicia when it was pointed out that Cosell had knocked her husband, "we didn't pay much attention to things such as that then. When people got very critical or attacked Tommy, we just considered the source."[5]

He hasn't changed a lot over the years. But he has become more outward than he was when he first took over the Cowboys. He was the youngest head coach who ever had been in the NFL and was taking over a new expansion team. It was the most difficult job anybody had ever had, and it took his full concentration. He did the job too.

But he was never that cold, stoic person people liked to paint him as being. He's a very warm person with a great sense of humor. I think most very intelligent people are witty.

The children always loved him so much. He was better with them when they were growing up than I was. He just kept calm and had a great understanding.[6]

—*Alicia Landry*

4

Landry and His Men

~

THEY SAW him cry a few times. Can you imagine, one of football's greatest coaches, crying? The times recalled were during desperate days for the team, the years when nothing in that oddball offense was clicking, or so it seemed to the man who designed it.

He'd stand before the team meeting, tears literally rolling down his cheeks, and say something about how this just didn't seem like it would work and he didn't know why. Then, in an act of desperation for him, Tom Landry would turn and walk out.

This was confusing to his men, who saw so little emotion in this stoic figure. They had never had a coach like this, who didn't yell after losses, but would pick them to pieces after victories.

He never got too personal with any of them during their playing days, but when a guy was hurt badly, such as in a car wreck, there was that hat—the fedora—by the bedside. There was Coach praying with their momma. There was Coach, leading Sunday devotional time, but never shoving Jesus down their throats.

To this day, many acquaintances get nervous just calling him on the phone, yet his influence in the areas of discipline and patience and preparedness have spread across business, family life, and football for the men who have called him Coach.

He sobbed the day he said good-bye to his team after the firing. The players were crying, too, in that private meeting. He addressed them and walked away, forever in a sense.

"Landry," said Danny White, "had such an impact on my life, my life with him ended when I didn't play for him anymore. Everything I do, he influences me to this day."

That was Coach. These are his men.

With all we learned from him, about football and life—being prepared— he was a huge impact, just a huge impact on thousands of young men.

—*Bob Lilly*

He influenced me to where I think about him all the
time. I find myself in a situation as a coach and I
wonder what Coach Landry would have done. Like if
there's a family situation, I wonder what Dad would
have done. If it's something with a player or football, I
ask what Coach Landry would have done.

When I was interviewing for head coach, they'd
say (in several cities), "Well, you've only been in the
Dallas system." There couldn't be a better system,
because he ran it.

—Dan Reeves

He is a fabulous person of high values and high standards who taught us how to make long-term plans with
a value system and a set of goals. He set long-term goals
for the team on defense and offense. At the time, I
thought that was kind of stupid, and as I got into business I knew he wasn't stupid at all.

—Bob Lilly

Coach Landry is the only professional coach I ever coached for. But he is one of the most fair people as far as handling his players. If you were a veteran, you had a place on that team and you had to lose your job.

—*Walt Garrison*

The last time I saw him was at an FCA banquet. He looked worn out. He'd had pneumonia and had been in the hospital ten or eleven days. He was diagnosed with leukemia right after that. He seemed kind of sad. His speech was kind of, well, like maybe he'd had a stroke.

It makes me feel like I'm not invincible. It makes me sad because he was always a strong person, a World War II pilot, a coach. He sold life insurance (in the off-season) in New York with a speech impediment and a Texas drawl because he needed a way to feed his family, and he became a member of the million-dollar round-table.

It shows we all have a certain amount of time. I hope he overcomes this (illness). I'd hate to lose a person of his magnitude.

—*Bob Lilly*

When Dad died, he [Landry] came to the funeral and he
didn't have to. He didn't get real close to you, but he
was always there when something personal happened.

—Walt Garrison

He was such a man of character and integrity. I
admired him so much. My dad was a farmer, a man of
integrity and a Christian. They were so much the
same—here my dad a farmer in south Alabama and
Coach Landry.

You didn't have to know Tom to see he lived with
integrity and honesty. That example has followed me
into business to this day. I think it made a lot of us
more successful.

—Lee Roy Jordan

He told us the total image of the Dallas Cowboys was
tied to our personal image.

—Bob Lilly

I was behind all my college peers in business when I came out of football. But the training I got from him was invaluable. It was sort of like a master's degree that lasted fourteen years.

—*Bob Lilly*

I think Tom Landry has had the greatest effect on my life of anyone I ever met in football. Maybe the most important thing I learned from him, the thing that will stay with me forever, is that it makes no sense to panic, to lose your poise and composure. That never helps, and on the other hand, there is always a solution, always some positive action you can take. I consider myself a lucky, lucky man to have known him and worked with him.[1]

—*Roger Staubach*

Lord, I love that old man.

—*Bob Lilly*

It just wasn't his personality to be emotional and friendly to us. I think he knew he couldn't keep his objectivity and be close to us. I think he might have liked to, but he couldn't do that and be successful.

—*Lee Roy Jordan*

I think Tom demonstrated a man can be dedicated to a job and a family. Everybody picked up on that and each one of us took a little of Tom into our lives.

—*Chuck Howley*

It just killed him to cut people, especially veterans, and I know he'd keep some guys around a year or two longer than another coach might have, but somehow it always worked out. Maybe the players knew how far out on a limb he had gone for them, and they found a way to perform, if only for one more critical moment in one more game.[2]

—*Doug Todd, longtime Cowboys publicist*

I remember one day, it's the morning of the game, and we're all sittin' in the locker room, maybe half an hour before we go out, real quiet like . . . just thinkin', gettin' ourselves ready to play, and in the stadium magazine that day there was some article on me as a bass fisherman, with a picture of me carryin' a string of, I don't know, thirty or forty bass that I'd caught, just carryin' them over my shoulder.

Now remember, it's like minutes before the game, and I'm not talkin' to anybody, just sittin' at my locker, my head still, picturin' stuff. So I'm sittin' there, he walks over to me, slaps me on the shoulder and says, "Hey Randy, that's a nice picture of you in that magazine, real nice."

I mean, he had to think I was retarded, because I just looked at him, couldn't say nothin', because he never talked to me before about anything but football, you know? I mean, tellin' me I looked good in a picture with a mess of fish hanging on my shoulder, right before a game? I mean, who's nuts around here, you know?

—*Randy White*

"Tom will always be remembered as a hero," said Tex Schramm, former Dallas Cowboys president who now heads the World League of American Football. "That's the way it should be."[3]

⌒

I miss Coach Landry. I used to look for him in the morning, and it became a regular part of the day, just seein' him, knowing he was there.

—*Bob Lilly*

⌒

My first impression of Coach Landry, my initial perception of him, was that of a top commanding officer. He had a presence, an aura, and people just naturally listened to him, watched him, took their lead from him. You always see other coaches go off, just like players, but Tom never did. I always wondered about that, and envied him, and respected him because of it.[4]

—*Roger Staubach*

⌒

You might say I learned to play linebacker while sitting in the Landry suite at the hotel. I'd be there in my room, you know, after practice, relaxing, and the phone would ring and it would be Tom.

"Sam," Landry would say, "what are you doing?"

"Oh, hello, Coach. Just resting, sitting here watching television. Kinda caught up in this show."

"Good, I'm glad you aren't doing anything. Why don't you come up to my room and look at some football films with me? There's some things I want to show you."

Tom had this projector in his apartment, and we'd go over the team we'd be playing that week, over and over . . . tendencies, what to look for, keys. I didn't get to finish watching a lot of interesting television programs that year, but I learned more football in that one season in Tom's apartment than I'd learned throughout high school and college.[5]

—*Sam Huff, Hall-of-Fame linebacker, recalling his rookie season with the Giants and young defensive coach Tom Landry*

**When I played for him, he was tough because he
wanted things to be done the correct way. I think
that's good. He didn't want anyone cheating themselves or cheating the team, and that's the way it
should be.**[6]

—Herschel Walker

I think the players, not the game, got away from Coach
Landry, because they just weren't the kind of players he
was used to seeing—to dealing with. Imagine, hair
dryers in the locker room.

—Bob Lilly

It got to where I'd feel comfortable enough to talk to
him. Not big important stuff, nothing really personal,
no small talk. I mean just sayin' hello to him first, in
the morning. I never even could do that when I first
came to Dallas. I tried once, said hello, and he just
walked right by me. He didn't do it to be rude, it's just
when he got to thinkin' about some football problem,
he didn't see and he didn't hear anything else.

—Randy White

THE NEXT MORNING I ANNOUNCED THE TRADE IN A SQUAD
MEETING, EXPLAINING I'D SPENT HOURS WITH DUANE [THOMAS]
TALKING ABOUT WHAT HE HAD TO DO TO BECOME PART OF THE
TEAM BUT THAT HE HAD REFUSED. I HAD NO CHOICE BUT TO
TRADE HIM.

BUT HAVING NO CHOICE DIDN'T KEEP ME FROM FEELING SICK
ABOUT IT. HERE WAS ONE OF THE GREATEST RUNNING TALENTS I'D
EVER SEEN COME INTO PROFESSIONAL FOOTBALL. WHAT BOTHERED
ME EVEN MORE THAN HIS WASTED TALENT WAS THE FACT THAT
DUANE WAS OBVIOUSLY A TROUBLED YOUNG MAN. HE NEEDED
HELP. AND I HADN'T BEEN ABLE TO GET THROUGH TO HIM.[7]

—Landry

We—all of us—had a relationship that was a little bit strange. We never became comfortable enough so that we were able to just call him to chat or visit. If I had something I thought he'd be interested in, or if there's something he could help me with, then I'd call him. And whatever it is, he'll do it. He always would, always did.

—*Lee Roy Jordan*

The big difference was Landry. He was the kicking coach, too, and would watch films of me kicking and pick up any flaws I had. He also studied Wietecha and Conerly, the center and holder, to see if they were doing anything wrong. He put it all together so we all had a good year kicking.[8]

—*Pat Summerall, one-time Giants kicker*

Actually, Tom Landry's got a great personality. I love the guy, but I don't spend much time with him.

—*Walt Garrison*

He didn't really include himself with the players when we won. It was like, "Well, I designed the right offense and I designed the right defense, and we scored points and stopped the other guys and that's why we won."

—*Lee Roy Jordan*

On Landry's most remarkable trait:

His work ethic, his preparation. I just always thought that there was no team we could ever come up against that could be more prepared, better prepared than we were. I was amazed, when I first came up, at his intelligence as a football coach. Hey, everybody can put X's and O's on a blackboard, but he knew situations . . . the short-yardage situations, goal-line, third-and-long . . . he could almost predict what could happen and I always found it amazing. You always see other coaches go off, just like players, but Tom never did. I always wondered about that, and envied him, and respected him because of it.[9]

—*Tony Dorsett*

I don't think he could get close and still make decisions about cutting players. Personally involved—emotionally involved—that wasn't what he wanted. He had to stay above the players, away from them, distant from them, in order to do what he felt was best for the Dallas Cowboys. No matter what.

I know Tom would much rather have had a friendly, close relationship with the players. But he didn't feel it would work for him, that he'd be able to maintain his objectivity.

—*Lee Roy Jordan*

I was never afraid of him. He was always the kind who never got real close to his athletes—always a thinking man, always preoccupied. He didn't have time. (But he was) a very warm man on the field. I never once heard him use a bad word except for *hell* and *damn*. But he could get angry, really angry. And he never got mad if we lost a game, but even when we won, he'd get outraged if we broke down, made a mental error, didn't do what the play called for us to do.

Everybody had some fear when it got to be Monday mornings, and we gathered together for the first review of the film of the game the day before.

Then we all knew he was going to jump on us. We knew it. No matter how well we did, we knew he wasn't going to be a happy man.

—*Bob Hayes*

They were all against Landry in the beginning. He lost like hell in those first five years and, to tell the truth, he'd probably have been sent packing just about anywhere else.

—*Walt Garrison*

I wanted to have that fear of him, that respect. It was both, you know. It was the kind of fear and respect you have for your father. You hate to bring that bad report card home. You hate to do anything wrong around him because you know he's gonna jump on you.

I wanted him to be up over me, I didn't want us to see eye to eye. I wanted that motivation through the fear of performing for him, playing a game on Sunday, and not knowing whether I did everything I could possibly do to keep him from jumping on me on Monday.

He never yelled, never raised his voice; always did it in a monotone.

—Drew Pearson

It was one of the ways that he used to teach football but some of us found could be applied to life, too. Like there's always a goal, one way or another, but you've got to have a method, a way of accomplishing that goal. I'm quite sure all of the players who have come through the system took that, at least, with them. It isn't enough just to set a goal, you have to come up with a method, a solution, a way to get it done.[10]

—Tony Dorsett

He's a good person, and once you get past his quiet, his distance, you understand where he's coming from. And he's a compassionate person, I know that for sure.

The night my father died—he died the night before we were playing Denver—well, I didn't say anything to anybody. I just kept it to myself, you know? That's my way. But I'll never forget, right before the game, as we were gettin' ready to be introduced in the tunnel, you know, he came over to me and said, "Sorry to hear about your father, and you take as much time as you need when you get back home, OK?"

Now, hell, he didn't have to do that, and it wasn't just me, it was a lot of people. When you had a real serious personal problem, you take all the time you need, do whatever you have to do, then come back.

—*Randy White*

He respected effort. He might not have thought you were going to be a superstar player for him . . . but he always respected desire and determination, and he truly believed that all you could do was your best, that no man could do any more than that.[11]

—*Roger Staubach*

I played for Bear Bryant at Alabama, and it was a
much more friendly relationship. He really was oppo-
site of Coach Landry. He motivated by [butt]-kickin',
[butt]-chewin', whatever. By fear in some cases. But he
also motivated by affection and love. He was a guy
who would get close to the players, but he was also the
guy who would get on you—I mean seriously get down
on you. I think Coach Landry kind of stayed away.
And by doing that he could discipline and motivate
without hurting himself by letting a player get too
close to him. He (Bryant) was more human, he didn't
mind showing you more affection than Coach Landry.
It was difficult for Coach Landry to show any feelings
whatsoever, because he couldn't turn it on and off and
I don't think he could be an effective coach without
acting the way he did.

—Lee Roy Jordan

As I wake up, the faces I remember seeing were my mother, Roger Staubach, Harvey Martin, and Coach Landry. And every time they'd wake me up after that, for a test or X-rays or something, or every time I'd just turn around and wake up on my own . . . they had me on a lot of heavy sedatives, you know . . . why, I'd see Coach Landry there. Every time, man. Every time. Every day. And I never thought he cared much about me . . . or any of the players.

It was kind of a revelation, man, because he was there, almost the whole time, day after day, until they knew I'd be all right.

—Drew Pearson, on a career-ending car accident
that killed his brother

Tom Landry had his priorities right. He knew what was important and what was just a waste of time, and if you look at things carefully in your own life, it's not hard to make the same decisions. That's one thing I learned from him . . . where to put the worry, where to put the importance.

Also, he taught me that you should never second-guess yourself, that once you make a decision don't worry about things you can't control. He surprised people who thought he was always so organized, so much under control, by sometimes making an important decision by the seat of his pants, so to speak. And once he made a decision, he never once went back to worry about it.[12]

—Doug Todd

I can call him now and feel comfortable, talk about other things besides X's and O's and football, talk about life. And that really didn't happen until after I stopped playing. But that was okay. I didn't need a coach who was going to be my buddy all the years I played.

What Tom Landry did for me was prepare me, week in and week out, to play football. I mean, the preparation we received, as athletes, was outstanding.

—*Drew Pearson*

Now and then too . . . for as long as I've known him, and before that, from talking to other players, there was always this about Tom Landry: If you needed him for something, he was there for you. If you needed help, advice, anything, he was ready to do whatever needed to be done, all the time. He has a great compassion about him, he cares about everybody he meets, and that's another part of him that only those who have spent a lot of time getting to know him have found out.[13]

—*Roger Staubach*

Dallas Cowboys players give Coach Landry a free ride after knocking off the Miami Dolphins, 24-3, in the 1972 Super Bowl. Rayfield Wright (No. 70), Mel Renfro (20), and Roger Staubach (12) are among the celebrants. (AP/Wide World Photos)

It was almost fitting, somehow, that after all the things we'd been through with this team, that his career would end so emotionally, so controversially. I mean, he could have retired, and there would have been stories for a couple of days. But this way, the mistreated old man who had won so many championships and Super Bowls. How can anybody do that? It went on for weeks, pages and pages of articles, and to me it was fantastic.

—*Lee Roy Jordan*

That (Landry's retirement ceremony in 1989) was the most embarrassed I've ever seen a man. I thought Tom was going to crawl under the carpet. This man was lauding Tom for his bombing. I believe Tom has lived in a pit of remorse and shame and guilt. He killed a lot of innocent people. You can say it was war, but killing is killing. How can you be a Christian and bomb?[14]

—*Thomas "Hollywood" Henderson*

It was shock and disbelief. I just couldn't imagine the Cowboys without Tom Landry.

—Drew Pearson

That 3-13 thing, that just, Lord, embarrassed him.
—*Lee Roy Jordan*

When it happened, and how it happened, I felt like a member of my family had died, like my mom or my dad.
—*Bob Hayes, on the firing of Tom Landry*

It brought tears to my eyes, that somebody could have brought so much to this organization and then just be thrown out like that. And not Tom Landry the *coach*, but Tom Landry the *person*. The man I got to know on a really personal basis. To learn that he really cared about his players, really felt for them, and just didn't know how to show it—or didn't think he should. Because when you get too close it might be tough to make the hard decision later, like cutting a guy, trading him, or just telling him it's probably time for him to retire. He deserved to be treated better than that, man. He really, really did, and whoever was at fault should be ashamed.
—*Drew Pearson*

I guess if you can fire
Tom Landry, you can
fire anyone.

—Lee Roy Jordan

5

Landry and Faith

~

AT A TIME when it wasn't as trendy to proclaim oneself as a born-again Christian or believer, or even to have a deep sense of values and morals, Landry did. He still does.

His life remains an amazingly accurate depiction of a perfect Christian life, or, for that matter, an impeccable value system that could be tied to the finest examples of many faiths.

However, Landry was every bit a Christian, which was made for hard walking on the landscape of his extremely analytical mind.

There is a good story about Landry, who he was, what his faith was about. It wasn't about bedsides of players in the hospital or trips to funeral homes when

the man they thought was aloof, sat at the casket of a
player's dead father.

Maybe it wasn't even that he went to Bible study
every Thursday.

Or that while other members of Highland Park
United Methodist Church were sneaking out early—or
not going at all—to see the kickoff so many Sundays—
the most worshiped sports figure in Dallas-Fort Worth
history was in the stands at one of God's stadiums. (And
that would not be the one with the hole in it).

If he could be there he would go to the early service.

Now, while there are many true Christians who
smoke, drink, and cuss now and then, it was not
Landry's way, other than an occasional *hell* and *damn*
near the line of scrimmage. And, indeed, he would
sometimes have a single Scotch.

A group of Dallas sportswriters was always seeking
to get at Landry, but in a fun way.

He was a hard one to pull a prank on, because he
sometimes didn't get it. Not because he wasn't clever.
He was every bit intelligent. But the darn guy was
always so intense thinking about football, whatever,
humor often blew right by him.

This one particular time was at a getaway that included writers, coaches, etc., for fishing, drinking, etc.

So these sportswriters figure they'll really "get" Landry and they go to his cabin for their nightly poker party—translated: gamblin', smokin', drinkin', cussin', etc.—and Landry walks into the common area of his cabin and sees a whole lot of stuff he doesn't do.

They laugh and invite Coach to play. Landry was nonplussed. He said no thanks and began to walk to his room. Well, Coach, if you're not going to play, then you can tend bar. And the man did, until right before daylight when he took a nap and went fishing.

That is a good-natured, loving man.

That is what they call "in the world but not of it."

He counseled players; gave drugged-out, coked-up guys third chances; acted as a character witness at their DWI trials. That is why they call him patient.

There are many people in sports who talk about their faith—and walk the walk occasionally. But usually there are breakdowns.

Landry is a sinner, just because the big playbook he lives by says everyone is. But to a man, of those interviewed, ask them to name a sin Landry committed.

They can't come up with a whole lot.

No matter what you believe, Landry's life makes it hard to deny that a life in Christ lived as he has lived it produces some awesome results. His life and career are a powerful testimony.

He wasn't one to preach religion to ya, but he lived it. I think any person that lives a godly life is a good example to anybody, and we looked up to Coach Landry for that. God was not a convenience for him. He didn't shove religion on you, but he wasn't ashamed of showing how religious he is.

—*Walt Garrison*

I was with him in the lean years with Meredith and those guys. I have seen him since he has had cancer and he remains cheerful in the midst of a lot of suffering.

—*Ken Dickson, Landry's pastor*

I felt very comfortable. I came from a hardcore background, Assembly of God. But Tom never pressured you. He impressed his faith on you by how he lived his life. I admired him for his stance. Few things were important to Tom Landry but Christ, family, and football, and, by golly, that made an impression on us.

—*Lee Roy Jordan*

AFTER THE 1958 SEASON I RETURNED TO
DALLAS. I WAS THIRTY-THREE YEARS OLD. I HAD
ACHIEVED ALMOST EVERY GOAL I HAD AIMED
FOR AND HAD EVERY REASON TO BE HAPPY AND
CONTENT. YET, INEXPLICABLY, THERE WAS AN
EMPTINESS IN MY LIFE . . .

"IS NOT LIFE MORE THAN FOOTBALL?" I
ASKED MYSELF, UNCOMFORTABLY. CHALLENGED
BY THIS STATEMENT, I TURNED MY THOUGHTS TO
THE CHALLENGER. WHO WAS HE, THIS JESUS?
DID I ACCEPT HIM, REALLY? FOR, I REASONED,
IF I ACCEPTED HIM, THEN I ACCEPTED WHAT
HE SAID. AND IF I ACCEPTED WHAT HE SAID,
THEN THERE WAS SOMETHING UNSATISFYING IN
THE WAY I WAS LIVING MY LIFE.

I BEGAN READING ABOUT JESUS.

—*Landry, in* Guideposts *magazine*

The thing I always admired was he walked the walk.
He didn't have to talk the talk. You just knew it. He
would just mention subtly that it says in the Bible this
is what you should do. He didn't pound it into you that
this is what a Christian should be.

—*Dan Reeves*

When somebody asks him to do something impromptu,
those are uneasy times for Coach Landry. I know he
hates public speaking. Yet he does it because he feels it
is important. He speaks at countless FCA banquets.
He's done TV commercials. He hates it. I really believe
his faith gets him through it.

—*Danny White*

He is a winner against odds. He just has this confidence. Quietness and confidence will be your strength.

—*Ken Dickson*

His Christian influence on all of us was probably the number-one thing he gave us. His values came from his faith, they were intermingled with it—God first, family second, football third. I remember him standing in the rain one day, the sun was out. It was funny, because he was walking on water.

—*Bob Lilly*

He didn't force his religion on anybody, but he had a strong belief in the Lord and wanted everybody to come to God. I'm Catholic and it made my faith stronger watching him. He has faced tragedy (his daughter's death), and I don't think Tom gets bitter at the Lord.

—*Chuck Howley*

"I've never written to a sportswriter before . . . " Landry (wrote), thanking me for "explaining (his) faith so accurately."

—*Skip Bayless, author of* God's Coach

GOD DOESN'T INTERFERE. WE HAVE GREAT CHRISTIAN FRIENDS AROUND THE LEAGUE. HE JUST GIVES YOU THE COURAGE TO EXCEL, THE CONFIDENCE TO PERFORM TO THE BEST OF YOUR ABILITY. SO MANY PEOPLE DON'T USE WHAT THEY'VE GOT. IT'S HOW YOU THINK THAT MAKES YOU SUCCESSFUL. IF YOU HAVE A POSITIVE ATTITUDE, GOOD THINGS WILL HAPPEN. WHY HAS POSITIVE THINKING BECOME A MILLION-DOLLAR INDUSTRY? THEY'RE JUST TEACHING WHAT GOD GIVES US IN THE BIBLE.[1]

—Landry

I COULD HAVE A BAD SEASON AND BE FIRED. I WOULD SUFFER. I'M HUMAN. THAT'S WHY THERE IS A GREAT NEED FOR GOD. I WOULDN'T STAY DOWN TOO LONG. I'D KNOW HE HAD SOMETHING ELSE IN MIND FOR ME OTHER THAN FOOTBALL.[2]

—Landry

I grew up Christian, but his example got me back to it. Some of the guys weren't necessarily Christian. We were in our twenties, half crazy, and he was the cement that kept some from going off the deep end. We learned how to handle ourselves. We were never told to read the Bible or accept the Lord or whatever. He would just mention how the Bible said this or that about something. For a lot of guys, it was the first they'd ever heard of it.

—*Bob Lilly*

When the church needed him, he was there. He was there every Sunday if he could be when he was in town. Other people in the congregation would hurry out early or not come at all when the Cowboys were playing. I'd kinda hurry the sermon up myself.

But the coach was there for the early service. Some minister was there one day, and he noticed Tom and Alicia walking down for communion, kneeling there together, and he noted that is what he thinks about when he thinks of Tom Landry, kneeling, just this picture of perfect humility.

—*Ken Dickson*

I CAN'T POINT TO A SPECIFIC MOMENT OR A SPECIFIC TIME WHEN I HAD A SUDDEN "BORN-AGAIN" EXPERIENCE. FOR ME, COMING TO MY OWN PERSONAL FAITH IN GOD TOOK PLACE OVER A PERIOD OF MONTHS IN 1959 (AFTER A FRIEND INVITED HIM TO A PRAYER BREAKFAST). BUT I FINALLY REACHED A POINT WHERE FAITH OUTWEIGHED THE DOUBTS, AND I WAS WILLING TO COMMIT MY ENTIRE LIFE TO GOD.[3]

—Landry

He put together a religion of the heart and of the mind. He'd go to Bible study every Thursday. He has always studied the Bible a lot, but not just the Bible—books on aeronautics, too.

—Ken Dickson

Above all, Tom was a practical man. He knew you could pray all you wanted, but if you can't play football, you're gonna get your [butt] beat on Sunday. Amen.

—Walt Garrison

WHILE I'LL ALWAYS HAVE MORE TO LEARN ABOUT APPLYING THE
BIBLE'S TEACHING TO MY DAILY LIVING, THE PRIORITIES LESSON
I'D LEARNED AS A NEW CHRISTIAN CONTINUED TO AFFECT ME. I
OFTEN LET FOOTBALL BECOME MORE THAN A CAREER TO ME—IT
WAS SOMETIMES AN OBSESSION. AS I BEGAN TO UNDERSTAND
WHAT THE BIBLE TAUGHT ABOUT LOVING GOD AND MY FAMILY, IT
HELPED ME PUT FOOTBALL IN PERSPECTIVE. WHILE IT DIDN'T
MEAN I WANTED TO WIN ANY LESS, I REALIZED WHATEVER I DID
OR DIDN'T ACCOMPLISH AS COACH OF THE COWBOYS WASN'T THE
MOST IMPORTANT THING IN MY LIFE. AND THAT HELPED TAKE
SOME OF THE PRESSURE OFF.[4]

—Landry

I don't think he asks, "Why me, Lord?" If he is ever
bitter, I guess that's between him and the Lord.
    *—Ken Dickson, on tragedy and failure, including the death of
                                    Landry's grown daughter.*

"Reverend T. L."

—Buddy Dial's nickname for Tom Landry

I HAD BEEN PRAYING AND ASKING GOD FOR SOME SORT OF DIREC-
TION AND GUIDANCE ABOUT MY FUTURE. AND NOW IT SEEMED I
HAD MY ANSWER. I TOOK THAT REMARKABLE TEN-YEAR CON-
TRACT AS CLEAR INDICATION OF GOD'S WILL FOR MY LIFE. AND I
NEVER AGAIN DOUBTED THAT COACHING WAS TO BE MY LIFE'S
CALLING.[5]

—Landry

PERSONALLY, THE LORD HAS MEANT A GREAT DEAL TO ME. I
BECAME A CHRISTIAN ONE YEAR BEFORE I TOOK OVER THE
DALLAS COWBOYS AND HE'S BEEN WITH ME ALL THESE DAYS
HERE IN DALLAS AND [HAS] MEANT A TREMENDOUS AMOUNT
TO ME. . . .[6]

*—Landry, excerpted from his comments during
his induction into the Texas Stadium Ring of Honor*

"... we thank You for the close walk with Your Son Jesus Christ and the work Alicia and Tom Landry have done and the impact they've had not only on this city and this state, but the nation and the world. And as a new chapter in this book, the Landry life, opens we pray, Oh God, that You will uplift them and hold them and use them mightily as You have in the past ... [7]

—*Ret. USAF Gen. Richard F. Abel, President of the Fellowship of Christian Athletes, giving the invocation during Tom Landry Day*

As a football coach, I measure things in terms of results. During each game we keep a chart of the players' efficiency in carrying out their assignments. If most players perform well, we probably win the game. Therefore, I couldn't help thinking about Jesus in terms of what He did, of the results of His life. The impact of His life on the lives of countless millions down through the years is impressive and compelling.

—*Landry, in* Guideposts

Landry had a devotional every Sunday before the game. . . . Hell, I believe in God. I was raised to go to church and it was kinda nice, really. You'd go to the devotional, get a little peace of mind, eat a pre-game meal, and then go try to cripple forty other human beings.

—*Walt Garrison*

FINALLY, AT SOME PERIOD DURING THE SPRING
OF 1959, ALL MY INTELLECTUAL QUESTIONS NO
LONGER SEEMED IMPORTANT, AND I HAD A CURI-
OUSLY JOYOUS FEELING INSIDE. INTERNALLY, THE
DECISION HAD BEEN MADE. NOW, WHILE THE
PROCESS HAD BEEN SLOW AND GRADUAL, ONCE
MADE, THE DECISION HAS BEEN THE MOST
IMPORTANT OF MY LIFE. IT WAS A COMMITMENT
OF MY LIFE TO JESUS CHRIST, AND A WILLING-
NESS TO DO WHAT HE WANTED ME TO DO, AS
BEST I COULD, BY SEEKING HIS WILL THROUGH
PRAYER AND READING HIS WORD . . .

HE DIDN'T ASK ME TO GIVE UP FOOTBALL OR MY AMBITION TO BE THE BEST COACH IN THE BUSINESS, BUT TO BRING HIM INTO MY LIFE, INCLUDING FOOTBALL. I BEGIN EACH DAY NOW WITH A PERSON-TO-PERSON EFFORT TO CONTACT HIM.

"LORD, I NEED YOUR HELP TODAY WHEN WE MAKE SQUAD CUTS," OR "PLEASE GIVE ME THE RIGHT WORDS TO SAY TO THE COACHES AT OUR MEETING," OR "PLEASE HELP ME TO FORGET ABOUT FOOTBALL TODAY WHEN I'M WITH ALICIA AND THE CHILDREN."

—*Landry in* Guideposts

For God so loved the world, that he gave his only begotten Son, that whosoever believeth in Him shall not perish, but have everlasting life (John 3:16)

—Landry's favorite Bible verse

⌒

Not only was he comforting me but my mother . . . and my other brothers . . . praying with them . . . doing all those things to show his support . . . the kind of things nobody knew anything about.

—Drew Pearson, on Landry after the accident
that ended his career and killed his brother

⌒

But even when he got players who really had problems, Tom always thought he would make a difference in their lives. Not in their football careers, but in their lives. He was always a good Christian, and he never thought a guy was all bad, or that there was no chance to save a guy, to set him on the right path.

—Lee Roy Jordan

⌒

SURE, I'M A CHRISTIAN, AND IT (LOCKER-ROOM TALK) BOTHERS ME. BUT I COULD SAY THAT ABOUT A LOT OF PLAYERS, TOO. BUT BEING AROUND TEX (SCHRAMM), I KNOW IT'S JUST PART OF HIS SPEECH PATTERN, NOT MEANT TO BE TAKEN LITERALLY MUCH OF THE TIME. THAT'S THE PATTERN OF SPEECH IN MUCH OF OUR SOCIETY TODAY. PEOPLE OFTEN DON'T KNOW WHAT THEY'RE SAYING, WHAT THE WORDS MEAN. IT'S JUST A WAY FOR THEM TO EXPRESS THEMSELVES.[8]

—Landry

WHEN I GET OUT OF TOUCH WITH HIM, I FLOUNDER. POWER SEEMS TO EBB AWAY, AND THAT RESTLESS FEELING RETURNS. WHEN GOD IS IN CONTROL OF MY LIFE, THAT GNAWING SENSE OF DISSATISFACTION IS GONE.[9]

—Landry

THE ANSWER IS, I'M A CHRISTIAN. THAT'S
WHERE I LIVE. IT'S HARD FOR A SECULAR SOCI-
ETY TO HANDLE. IT'S A DIFFICULT THING TO
EXPLAIN. I DON'T WANT TO COME ACROSS AS A
PIOUS-TYPE PERSON. I SUFFER AFTER LOSSES,
BUT FORTUNATELY, I RECOVER QUICKLY. I HAVE
A SOURCE OF POWER I WOULDN'T HAVE WITH-
OUT MY RELATIONSHIP WITH CHRIST. I'VE
REACHED THE POINT WHERE I FEEL NO PRES-
SURE IN THE SUPER BOWL.[10]

—Landry

6

Landry and Football

~

IT STARTED in Mission, Texas, where a kid didn't really have to play well to play football, everybody just did. But Landry was good.

He grew up playing on a sandlot, devising plays. Then it was on to the University of Texas to play fullback. People took notice of the Orange Bowl's top rusher.

He was known as the guy who studied films more than the bottom of cocktail glasses and the hems of well-formed miniskirts.

He became a coach, with Vince Lombardi, for the New York Giants, under Jim Lee Howell.

Howell called him the greatest coach in the NFL early on, and that alone became the foundation for the myth. He then began formulating a new theory that left nowhere to go, as some call it. It is really called the Flex, a defense viewed as revolutionary in the 1950s.

He began issuing IQ tests to those with a decent time in the forty. It took thinkers to run his schemes.

Yes, they call him a genius.

A lot of it was hard work.

All that film-studying defined him. That, and the fact he was always so focused on the game that he hardly saw people in the hall in the mornings.

Ah, but the films. He watched them to the point he knew if an opposing player stepped off his right or left foot at the line of scrimmage—and how to use that to his team's advantage.

Dallas had a very complicated offense. Motion and divide—the famous Landry, multiple offense. On a pass route, for example, if you were weak-side back, you'd run a circle. If you were strong-side back, you'd run a straight route. The strong side was where the wingback lined up, but if he went in motion then that was suddenly the weak side. If you're a little confused, I don't blame you, because I know I sure was.

—Walt Garrison, on his rookie season

What he learned was amazing. Then he taught it to us. Everything I got as a coach was from him.

—Dan Reeves

I can remember times when things (not good ones) happened on the field. And he always handled those with great compassion as a person. Most coaches rant and rave and that's the last thing you need as a player.

—Danny White

Few people realize what a great coach he is. Most
coaches should be worshiping at his feet.

—*Frank Gifford*

When we lost a game (bad) one time, I'd find myself
thinking how Coach Landry would be disappointed in
me. He is the measuring stick for me. He was the greatest
teacher ever to coach in the National Football League.

—*Dan Reeves*

Tom is such a difficult guy to describe. All business. All
coach. He kept his distance because he was afraid he
couldn't be objective. Sometime I want to call him, but
I feel like I'm putting him out. Most of us feel that way.
There was a certain persistence.

—*Lee Roy Jordan*

He was about the most organized person ever. Everything we did—there was a reason it was done. He was a stickler for details and anything you gave him that was a new idea, you better have the facts to back it up.

—*Dan Reeves*

There was so much he was responsible for, God, so much. He was learning to be a head coach when he was young, and the way he was, was the only way he knew how to do it.

—*Lee Roy Jordan*

He did not yield when it came to execution. He'd tell you how you screwed up, but I never thought he wanted to embarrass anybody.

—*Danny White*

He always made sense to me. I gained a real apprecia-
tion for what he accepted as a head coach. More than
anything, the impact he had on the players. I find
myself today asking, "What would Coach Landry do?"
Not just the X's and O's, but in dealing with players,
what would Coach Landry do?"

—Danny White, head coach, Phoenix Rattlers

We had a good team because we had great athletes, but
lots of teams had that. What we had was Coach Landry
and his preparation and his brain and all the stuff
nobody else had or ever could have. And the more
things he said that came out right, the more you
believed him next week. Most teams in this league
have the talent to play about the same, see, but it was
Landry, his ability to coach, to be innovative, that
brought us up to a higher level.

—Drew Pearson

I've known a lot of good coaches, but Coach Landry went beyond being a great coach to [also] being a great teacher of people.

—*Danny White*

MY FIRST PROFESSIONAL START CAME AGAINST (THE CLEVELAND BROWNS) BECAUSE OF AN INJURY TO ONE OF OUR STARTING DEFENSIVE BACKS. AND (CLEVELAND OWNER-COACH) PAUL BROWN AND (HALL-OF-FAME BROWNS' QUARTERBACK) OTTO GRAHAM KNEW A RAW ROOKIE WHEN THEY SAW ONE. THEY THREW AT ME ALL DAY. (ALL-STAR) RECEIVER MAC SPEEDIE TURNED ME INSIDE OUT AND LEFT ME OUT TO DRY. HE SET THE OFFICIAL AAFC SINGLE-GAME RECORD FOR RECEIVING THAT DAY—WELL OVER TWO HUNDRED YARDS.

THAT GAME WAS THE SINGLE MOST EMBARRASSING ATHLETIC PERFORMANCE OF MY ENTIRE LIFE. BUT IT ALSO PROVED TO BE ONE OF THE MOST IMPORTANT. BECAUSE THE PRIMARY LESSON I LEARNED THAT DAY, REINFORCED OVER THE NEXT FEW YEARS, SERVED AS THE VERY FOUNDATION OF MY PHILOSOPHICAL APPROACH TO PLAYING AND COACHING FOOTBALL. I REALIZED MY OWN LIMITATIONS. I CONCEDED THAT IT WAS IMPOSSIBLE TO SUCCEED SOLELY ON SKILL, ON EMOTION, OR EVEN ON DETERMINATION. ANY SUCCESS I EVER ATTAINED WOULD REQUIRE THE UTMOST IN PREPARATION AND KNOWLEDGE . . .

THAT DAY IN CLEVELAND WAS THE STARTING POINT, THE BEGINNING OF THE CHALLENGE TO REALLY LEARN THE GAME OF FOOTBALL.[1]

—Landry

One of the hardest workers I ever met.

—Danny White

He was a great listener. Very much a great listener. That is one of the weaknesses I have, to listen and not interrupt. To listen and decide yes or no and not make you feel bad.

—Dan Reeves

Tom and Vince were both tremendous coaches and people. On the surface Vince was a warmer person than Tom. He went from warm to red hot. You could hear him laughing or shouting for five blocks. You couldn't hear Landry sometimes if he was sitting in the next chair. Lombardi was more of a teacher, whereas Landry seemed like a professor. It was as though Tom lectured the top 40 percent of the class and Vince the lower 10 percent.[2]

—the late Wellington Mara, New York Giants owner, comparing his former assistant coaches

Coach Landry was the last person in the world I wanted to see when I came off the field. That was probably the worst I felt about anything I've done (audibling a punt to a fake kick and running short of a first down). I wanted to avoid him, but, sure enough, he came over to me when I got back on the bench.

"Danny," Landry said, calmly, "you just can't do that. You just can't do that."

I was worried the next week and got a little paranoid when I felt he wasn't talking to me. But that was all just in my mind. Coach Landry doesn't hold grudges against anybody, not even some of the people who over the years have really betrayed or disappointed him.[3]

—*Danny White*

"That's a good catch, Walt," he says, then turns around and says to me, "but don't ever drop one." Believe me, that's the last hot-dog catch this Cowboy ever made.

—*Walt Garrison*

Landry left the telephone, caught up with his family on the course, and played golf until near darkness, as if nothing were wrong (the day of his impending firing). Tom was waiting on the street by the club when (Jerry) Jones and (Tex) Schramm arrived and went, along with his son, into a nearby sales office to talk.

"If you're just coming down here for a publicity stunt, you need not have bothered."

At first there was this certain look in his eyes, on his face, that he gets when he's mad. And then, if you knew him, you could tell, he was feeling emotional too.

It was the most inadequate I've ever felt. I [Jerry Jones] want to assure everybody who is interested in the Cowboys, and certainly in Coach Landry, that he saw my baby blue eyes as quickly as humanly possible under the circumstances. . . I was so sensitive to his feelings . . . I was basically trying to say something that couldn't be said. He was magnificent to me for what he had been through. He's special.[4]

He had a tremendous insight into three years from now. And a tremendous patience with people.

—*Dan Reeves*

The respect for him was unbelievable on the staff. Yet we didn't have that closeness.

—Dan Reeves

He never forgets anything.

About six years ago when we were playing Chicago I tried to run with a punt I'd caught inside our ten. It was late in the game and I knew I should have fair caught it, but I just thought I'd run upfield as far as I could, then step out of bounds and stop the clock. I got hit near the sidelines, fumbled, and Chicago recovered. I looked up and there was Coach Landry standing over me looking directly into my eyes.

Six years later I got back for a punt return against Chicago and he said, "Cliff, fair catch the ball. You remember what happened last time."[5]

—Cliff Harris

JUST BE RIGHT.

—Landry's advice to players who improvised on his plays

You know, he'd tell me Wednesday that when we were going to play . . . oh, say St. Louis . . . that when I did this kind of move the cornerback . . . like maybe Roger Wehrli, one of the best I played against . . . would back up with his right foot first, and if I took advantage of that, knowing which way he was going to back up, I could gain half a step from the first move. Now, I mean, this was Wednesday, man. How the hell did he know what the guy was going to do next Sunday?

—*Drew Pearson*

[Cowboys owner Clint] Murchison eased into Landry's peripheral vision just once to suggest a play. Murchison said, "You know Tom, if, uh, Frank Clarke is averaging seventeen yards on a reverse, well, shoot, you have to wonder how far a guy as fast as Bob Hayes could go if he ran one.

"Tom gave me all this mumbo jumbo about strong and weak side, and I nodded sagely and walked away."

Three or four games later, Murchison watched Hayes lose four yards on a reverse and said, "That's Tom's way of telling me to stay out of football."[6]

It took a few years before people began to believe the mumbo jumbo Landry was throwing around. Especially the players. Now, if they'd known Landry was going to fashion the Cowboys into the winningest team in the NFL over the next twenty years, it would have been a lot easier to swallow all this weird crap Landry was trying to force-feed them. But when you lose 76 percent of your games the first four years like Landry did, it takes a farsighted individual to think you're anything but a crackpot with some [bad] ideas.

—*Walt Garrison*

He told me I didn't have great speed, but I had great moves and body control, so he said, "Drew, when you come off the line of scrimmage at the snap of the ball, why not pump those arms up and down—act like you're already at full speed." I thought about that, and it occurred to me that if I saved something, I could lull defensive backs to sleep. I had been a wide receiver in high school, in college, and now, getting to see the way Tom Landry looked at football, it was a whole new game.

—*Drew Pearson*

Religious man . . . the cap on his head, always . . . in meeting rooms . . . on the [black]board, going over each play, each position . . . offense, defense, the kicking game . . . and he was knowledgeable about each and every position. You could ask him a question for a variation on those plays and he would immediately turn around and answer, spontaneously. The answers were always there, because he had thought about all the possible variations and solved the puzzle before you even had a chance to think of one small adjustment.

—*Bob Hayes*

Landry's reaction to NFL Films editor Bob Ryan's titling the Cowboys' 1978 highlight film "America's Team":

AMERICA'S TEAM. THE MOMENT I HEARD IT I THOUGHT, OH, NO! EVERYBODY'S REALLY GONNA BE GUNNIN' FOR US NOW. I DON'T KNOW ANYONE ON THE COWBOYS WHO LIKED THE LABEL TO START WITH. SO MANY NEWSPAPERS PICKED UP ON IT THAT OTHER TEAMS USED IT AS A MOTIVATIONAL TOOL AGAINST US. HOWEVER, WHAT SEEMED SO PRESUMPTUOUS AT FIRST EVENTUALLY BECAME PART OF THE PROUD COWBOYS' TRADITION.[7]

I wasn't surprised that there was so much emotion. But I think the breadth and depth of feelings for Coach Landry were more than anybody imagined. I would have been more concerned if there had been apathy. I'm deeply glad for the way the fans responded to Coach Landry.

I guess I'll always be thought of as the Darth Vader in this situation.[8]

—Jerry Jones

The coach reflected on charges of "senility" that surfaced after a call he made in a 1988 Cowboys loss to the Eagles:

SENILITY WOULD HAVE HELPED ME IGNORE THE RAGE OF CRITICISM THAT ROSE AROUND ME. I HADN'T SEEN OR HEARD SO MUCH FLAK SINCE THOSE WORLD WAR II BOMBING RUNS OVER GERMANY. JUST AS THEN, I HAD TO SET MY MIND ON THE TASK AND PRESS ON.[9]

—*Landry*

Landry's final words to his players, following his 1989 firing by Jerry Jones:

THE WAY YOU REACT TO ADVERSITY IS THE KEY TO SUCCESS. PEOPLE WHO SUCCEED ARE THE ONES WHO RESPOND THE RIGHT WAY IN ADVERSE CIRCUMSTANCES. RIGHT NOW . . . THINGS ARE IN TURMOIL AROUND HERE . . . HOW YOU REACT WILL BE CRUCIAL . . . IMPORTANT TO WHAT HAPPENS NEXT SEASON. I DON'T WANT YOU TO CONCERN YOURSELF WITH WHAT HAS HAPPENED TO ME . . . YOU NEED . . . TO LOOK FORWARD . . . TO PLAYING FOOTBALL NEXT SEPTEMBER. . . . I WANT YOU GUYS TO DO EVERYTHING YOU CAN TO BRING THE COWBOYS BACK TO THE TOP OF THE NFL."[10]

Tom Landry's wearing a headset never would have worked. For one thing, it would have meant having to remove the fedora. Quarterbacks Danny White and Glenn Carano flank Landry during a 1980 game against the Rams. (AP/Wide World Photos)

7

Landry and Fashion

~

ALICIA USUALLY bought his clothes. In a sense they were an outward and visible sign of who he was in the Christian sense as well as in the business sense.

Always looking like he had come straight from the early service. Many times he had.

He wanted his players looking the same way—well, maybe without that hat.

Some kids who grew up in Dallas felt their dads were not up to a certain amount of, well, respect, if they didn't wear a fedora to work—and that's the truth.

Years after his firing, he appeared at a charity golf event in shorts, and one of those short-sleeved dress shirts like dads wear. Then there were the tube socks pulled up as far as they could go, then the Sperry Topsiders.

It didn't look like Landry.

His image in fashion was etched so deeply into the collective Dallas-Fort Worth psyche, it was as if he was expected to wear a dress hat and a suit to the country club.

SOMEWHERE ALONG THE LINE I DEVELOPED AN IMAGE ALL MY OWN. I DIDN'T CAMPAIGN FOR THE TITLE OF "THE MAN IN THE HAT." BUT I GOT IT.

IT ALL STARTED BACK IN NEW YORK, ACTUALLY. AS AN ASSISTANT COACH OF THE GIANTS, WITH PLANS TO GO INTO BUSINESS AFTER FOOTBALL, I DECIDED I SHOULD TRY TO LOOK SUCCESSFUL AND BUSINESSLIKE ON THE SIDELINE. IT CAN GET COLD IN NEW YORK DURING FOOTBALL SEASON, AND HATS WERE IN FASHION AT THE TIME, SO A NICE FEDORA SEEMED THE FINISHING TOUCH TO MY WORKING WARDROBE.

WHEN I CAME TO DALLAS OUR FIRST COWBOYS TEAMS WERE SO BAD I FELT IT EVEN MORE IMPORTANT TO AT LEAST LOOK SUCCESSFUL. A LOT OF PEOPLE SUGGESTED I SWITCH TO A COWBOY HAT, BUT THAT SEEMED TOO TRITE. I STUCK WITH MY TRADITIONAL SIDELINE ATTIRE.

MY HATS DID GIVE ME AN IDENTITY. IN FACT, IF I HAD A DOLLAR FOR EVERY TIME SOMEONE HAS SEEN ME BAREHEADED AND SAID, "I ALMOST DIDN'T RECOGNIZE YOU WITHOUT YOUR HAT ON," I COULD HAVE BOUGHT THE COWBOYS MYSELF.[1]

—Landry

How we looked was very important to Coach Landry.

—Bob Lilly

~

He was so much more than the man in the hat.

—Chuck Howley

~

An apparently discontent Landry goes casual during a practice at London's Crystal Palace preceding the 1986 American Bowl game against the Chicago Bears. (AP/Wide World Photos)

I'VE JUST ALWAYS DRESSED THIS WAY. I'VE ALWAYS
ENJOYED WEARING HATS AND FELT COMFORT-
ABLE IN THEM. A HAT FINISHES OFF A COACH'S
DRESS ON THE SIDELINES. IT'S IMPORTANT FOR A
TEAM TO DRESS WELL BECAUSE HOW YOU DRESS
AND LOOK HAS SOMETHING TO DO WITH YOUR
ATTITUDE AND SUCCESS ON THE FIELD. PLAYERS
TAKE PRIDE IN THEIR PERFORMANCES AND
SHOULD DO LIKEWISE IN THEIR CLOTHES.[2]

—Landry

8

Landry and "the Face"

 IT NEVER seemed to change. Oh, it might go vaguely from what really was a happy grin to the daggers of disappointments described by some.

It wasn't really a poker face, but it never seemed to change in victory or defeat—at church or at a speaking engagement. Don't misconstrue this; he had a smile and a grimace under that hat. Grandchildren were usually good for the former.

But what defines Landry's outward appearance as much or more as the hat and suit? The demeanor below the fedora, of course.

Tom Landry is someone you need to take at extreme face value. I do resent the business about Tom's [supposedly] being cold. He is a very passionate man. He doesn't do a lot of arm waving. He's just steadfast with a great power of will.

One of our friends had a child who was physically disadvantaged and someone told Tom about it. I took him over there to see the child, and I figured he'd sign an autograph and go. (As it turned out) I thought I'd never get him to leave. All this time he took for one person and there was no publicity involved. No one knew about it but us. He did a lot of things like that.

He is not cold.

—*Ken Dickson, Landry's pastor*

People may have disagreed with him, but I think they loved and respected him. Ours was always an unspoken relationship. Because of his personality, he always seemed a little distant. For the most part, Tom Landry is introverted to the point of being shy. The result was you often felt uneasy around him.

—*Danny White*

I took a few trips with him and I just love the way he smiles.

—*Ken Dickson*

I think Tom scared us all off, he was so quiet. We feared him because we knew he was right all the time. His mind would go a hundred miles an hour. I would walk into his office at camp and he was so focused, it would be two or three minutes before he knew I was standing there.

There are times I don't feel comfortable in his presence. I feel like I'm intruding.

—*Chuck Howley*

You always see other coaches go off, just like players, but Tom never did. I always wondered about that, and envied him, and respected him because of it.[1]

—*Tony Dorsett*

Since I've become a head coach, I
respect Coach Landry more than
ever. I always wondered why he was
so emotionless—why he didn't yell
when we scored or scream when
something went wrong. He looked at
the play and went right back to what
he was doing—it didn't take me long
to realize you can't do that (get
emotional). You have to separate
yourself from what's happening on
the field. Once it's happened, that's
it. Griping about it or cheering
about it, that's for the fans.

—*Dan Reeves*

Every year I had to get together the team Christmas video. I'll never forget. You know, everybody always talked about the face he had and the hats he wore. Well, he agreed to pose in this series of goofy hats and making these faces.

It was so hard for him to do that kind of stuff, but he would.

—*Danny White*

[Frank Gifford] would come do Monday night games and laugh about how people would say Tom was so intimidating. Gifford would say, "Why? Tom's a nerd. He's so shy, so square. Why does anyone think he's intimidating?"

— *Greg Aiello, former Cowboys public relations director*

If people had a hard time figuring out Landry's system, it was nothing compared with the trouble they had trying to figure out his personality.

—*Walt Garrison*

Description of Landry during the singing of the National Anthem at the city of Dallas celebration honoring him:

Landry stood there at attention, holding his hat in his hand over his heart. Tom Landry is the kind of person who still always gets chill-bumps when he hears the National Anthem.[2]

—*Bob St. John*

ONE REASON I SO SELDOM REACTED TO A BIG COWBOYS PLAY WAS BECAUSE I HARDLY EVER SAW ANY OF OUR OFFENSIVE PLAYS. I ALWAYS KNEW WHAT PLAY WE HAD CALLED; I DIDN'T HAVE TO WATCH IT. THE ONLY UNCERTAINTY WAS HOW THE OPPOSITION REACTED; IT WAS THEIR DEFENSE I NEEDED TO WATCH AND ANALYZE SO I WOULD KNOW BEST HOW TO COUNTER IT. AND ONCE A PLAY ENDED, I NEVER HAD TIME TO REACT, IMMEDIATELY SHIFTING FOCUS TO MY GAME PLAN TO DECIDE WHAT PLAY I SHOULD SEND IN NEXT.[3]

—*Landry*

I got further along in my career and started to realize that was just how he was. The feelings were there. The love was there, he just didn't let you see them. He kept everything so locked in, so reserved inside himself, that we never saw the feeling he had for the players.

—*Lee Roy Jordan*

He was a very intense, very driven man, and he made us play better than we ever thought we could.

—*Drew Pearson*

It's not a personality flaw in Landry that he shows no emotion on the sidelines. He's not cold. He's under control. Landry didn't encourage you to be emotional on the field. But he didn't discourage it either. Landry wasn't big on pep talks. He figured if you did your job, you'd win. And your job was to play football. So if he had to give you a pep talk to get you to do your job, then you shouldn't be there.

—*Walt Garrison*

I was watching in wonder as the coaches and staff around Landry ordered cocktail upon cocktail while Tom got lost in his game plan or one of his favorite Louis L'Amour novels.

—Skip Bayless, author of God's Coach

When all hell is breaking loose, he's the rock.

—Doug Todd, former Cowboys public relations director

He's forgotten I'm there. It's a completely meaningless game and I'm still on the bench. Finally, with about two minutes left in the game, we got the ball and Landry looks around and says, "Hey, you, get the ball." I don't think Landry knew my name the first three years I was with Dallas. It was always, "Hey you." So he points to me and I run on out there.

—Walt Garrison, recalling a game against Pittsburgh

You know, most people thought he was just that cold, rigid old man with the hat and the jacket, who never smiled. Including me, man, and I had been with him eleven years. Eleven years playing for the guy and never getting a feel that he cared so much for his players. My mother told me later how they would lean on him, how he would do things for them, make sure everything was OK. How he was a— oh, I know this sounds corny—how he was a pillar of strength for them when they were in need.

—Drew Pearson, on Landry's actions after Pearson's career ended in a car wreck that killed his brother

BUT MY POWER OF CONCENTRATION WAS JUST ONE OF THE REA-
SONS FOR THE UNFLAPPABLE REPUTATION I EARNED IN THOSE
EARLY YEARS OF FRUSTRATION AND CONTINUING LOSS. JUST AS
SIGNIFICANT WAS THE CONTINUING CONFIDENCE I HAD IN THE
SYSTEM. I KEPT TELLING MYSELF AND MY PLAYERS THAT WE'D KEEP
ON IMPROVING; IT WAS JUST A MATTER OF TIME, EXPERIENCE, AND
THE RIGHT PERSONNEL. AND OUR RECORD DID IMPROVE FROM NO
WINS IN '60, TO FOUR IN '61, AND FIVE IN '62.[4]

—Landry

Do you know, that [after the "Hail Mary" catch to beat
the Vikings] was the only time in all my years with the
Cowboys that Coach Landry ever hugged me. Yes sir.
He did. Now, it wasn't one of those wild, emotional
hugs, you know.

—Drew Pearson

It made me sick, watching the whole thing. The press was all over him, crowding him and asking him if he was going to lose his job. People were saying negative things about him and some of it was coming from his own organization. If you ask me, well, Coach Landry knew what he was doing but some other people in the organization were in a panic and choking. We were aware about all that stuff concerning a member or two of his staff not supporting him. All those things made it tougher on the players, too.

Then here you had Coach Landry just going on and trying to do his job. I tell you, if it had been me, I think I might have punched somebody in the nose.

Hey, maybe Coach Landry felt like that, too, but he never showed it.[5]

—*Randy White*

It seemed that (the look, the monotone) would always cut, always dig so much deeper. I wished the guy would yell at me. Just yell and scream and get it done with.

—*Drew Pearson*

I caught it in the clear at the twenty and had an easy touchdown. Thing was, when I got to the goal line and started to ease up, I could still hear Landry pounding after me, so I ran right through the end zone. He was still coming . . . I was ten yards beyond when he finally tackled me. Oh, he was [ticked] off. I was pretty hot myself by this time. I said, "Here! If you want it so bad, take it," and slammed the ball in his face. Then I scrambled up and ran for the bench because I knew I'd be safe there, and I'll be damned if he didn't chase me halfway to the bench.

—Former Rams receiver Glenn Davis,
as told by Skip Bayless

9

Landry and Love

⁓

 TOM LANDRY loved his players. He has been a man, those close to him say, with a great capacity to love. He just doesn't show it quite the way some people do.

When Landry happened to hug a player, which was rare, they were floored.

Sometimes they didn't know he knew their names, let alone loved them. But he did, with a great capacity to love the most unlovable even more in a sense.

He was shy in showing it to those outside his family. To have been affectionate to players would have put him in compromise. He showed it in other ways, helping their families in times of trial; heck, even going to trials of players in trouble.

In turn, most loved him back—at least by the time their playing days were over and they didn't have to sit through those Monday film sessions.

I think *love* is a big word. But, it is probably appropriate. I probably respected him more than I loved him. You love your teammates. You respect your coach. That was Coach Landry's way.

He did love people, though.

The hardest thing was when he cut a veteran. I never saw it, but they say he would cry.

—*Walt Garrison*

I'd have probably run in front of a car for that man.

—*Randy White*

He made us want to work harder and he coached out of love.

—*Danny White*

He wanted to be liked and loved, but I've seen other motivators and he was different.

—*Lee Roy Jordan*

You know when you leave home, you love your parents, but when you become one, you respect their decisions more. I respected and loved Coach Landry. What I've been through now, I really realize the tremendous job he did.

—*Dan Reeves*

I guess the one thing he did that surprised me a lot of ways was when Duane Thomas was not talkin' to anybody and he kind of reached out to Duane. He put up with Duane that whole year and that shocked a lot of players. He just wanted to save everybody and the deal with Duane Thomas said the most about that. He just saw that deep down, Duane was a good person and he didn't want him to fall through the cracks.

—*Walt Garrison*

I loved him.

—*Lee Roy Jordan*

Landry, at his Valley Ranch office in February 1989, contemplates his future after being informed by new team owner Jerry Jones that he no longer is coach of the Cowboys. (AP/Wide World Photos)

10

Landry and Motivation

~

 TOM LANDRY believed classic motivation was risky because the "rah rah" coaches who didn't have a lot of talented players could have the troops turn on them when all that screaming didn't translate into success.

And that's how he did it. Probably different than any coach in the history of the game.

Studying like a madman, and making his team the best prepared in the NFL.

[The] people who fired him [were] saying he doesn't motivate players, and he didn't pep talk 'em? You can believe one thing: He damn well motivated me. It was better than any pep talk I ever got in my life. All he had to do, you see, was embarrass me a little in front of my teammates. That's all he had to say to build a fire in me.

—Randy White

He had his way of being responsive and supportive, but he didn't make a show out of it. It was a quiet way, like he was in most things.

—Lee Roy Jordan

He never yelled. He could look at you. All you could do was see the disappointment in his eyes and it drove a dagger into your heart. He could do that, and you could still feel he cared about you. Kind of like some parents can do, and the kids know they are still loved.

—Danny White

At times I didn't realize what a great motivator he was.
When we walked on the field, we were totally prepared.

—*Dan Reeves*

MOST SUCCESSFUL PLAYERS NOT ONLY ACCEPT RULES AND LIMITA-
TIONS, I BELIEVE THEY NEED THEM. IN FACT, I BELIEVE PLAYERS
ARE FREE TO PERFORM AT THEIR BEST ONLY WHEN THEY KNOW
WHAT THE EXPECTATIONS ARE, WHERE THE LIMITS STAND.

I SEE THIS AS A BIBLICAL PRINCIPLE THAT ALSO APPLIES TO
LIFE, A PRINCIPLE OUR SOCIETY AS A WHOLE HAS FORGOTTEN:
YOU CAN'T ENJOY TRUE FREEDOM WITHOUT LIMITS.[1]

—*Landry*

He knew each guy on the team. When to be rough,
when to be calm. He just knew so much about you.
That was his style of doing things.

—*Randy White*

We're sitting there [in the Monday film sessions] and I'm thinking about guys from other teams, all around the country, sittin' in their meeting rooms, watching their films, and I'm wondering if they're catching the same kind of hell for losing that we were catching after we won. Probably not, you know? But that made us win, because guys on Sunday thought of that Monday morning session and we were just terrified to be singled out. He kept us always thinking, always on our toes, always off-balance somehow.

—*Bob Hayes*

There were guys who would throw up or get nauseated before going into those meetings.

—*Lee Roy Jordan on Landry's Monday player "critique"*

Sometimes if we were really stinking up the field he might come in and say, "This game plan is good. You're just not executing." But he never yelled, "Kill, kill, kill."

—*Walt Garrison*

I mean, we'd come in [on Monday] after winning a game by thirty points and he'd start in telling us what we did wrong. No compliment, no pat on the back. Just pointing out all our mistakes. That was his way. If you lost a game and you played poorly, he'd come in and he wouldn't be screaming or red in the face or anything. He'd just say softly, "You know such and such happened, and we just didn't play well," and then he'd just bow out after that.

—*Lee Roy Jordan*

He was a master of psychology. He knew how to motivate his players. And sometimes he motivated by fear. But it was strange, you know? We were never in fear of him, only of how he could be, of what he would say in front of everybody else. It was very strange, really. We liked him, but we were still afraid of the things he'd do.

—*Bob Hayes*

Coach Landry would go watch films for a day and a half
(after a loss) and then he'd come in and he'd have a
legal pad about nine feet long . . . I mean, he'd chew
[us out] for three hours for every mistake. And when he
was finished, I mean, the guy was devastated. I mean,
he chewed him out for every one of the mistakes. He
wouldn't let him off. But, you know, it was never personal. It was just his way of telling us what we did
wrong, because more than anything that man wanted
us to be perfect, to never make a mistake.

—*Lee Roy Jordan*

Sometimes—it's going to sound like I'm being critical
of Coach Landry, and I'm not—but sometimes I felt
like we worked too hard. Like we left a lot on the practice field a lot of times, and we'd go into games tired.
But then we'd be afraid of letting down because of him,
so we just couldn't let down.

I mean, playing for Coach Landry was not some
high school picnic, you know?

—*Randy White*

THE PRIMARY CHALLENGE OF COACH-ING IN THE NATIONAL FOOTBALL LEAGUE CAN BE BOILED DOWN TO A ONE-SENTENCE JOB DESCRIPTION: TO GET PEOPLE TO DO WHAT THEY DON'T WANT TO DO IN ORDER TO ACHIEVE WHAT THEY WANT TO ACHIEVE.[2]

—*Landry*

He used to get to me, man. I mean, in a
major way. And he did it for years and years.
And I knew when he was doin' it, and yet,
I'll guarantee you, he'd get me every time.
Every time. Like, we'd have a morning
meeting—and I used to take everything personally, and I knew what he was doing.

And he'd say something like, "Well,
things didn't go well in practice this
week"—or like, "We didn't play as well as I
know we can last Sunday," and I used to
think he was talking to me, just to me,
every time.

I'd take everything personally, and I'd
say something to myself like, "Wow, man,
what did I do wrong now?"

I mean, there were forty-three, forty-
five other guys there, and I felt like it was
all my fault.

He made me think I had lost the game, or damn near lost it, if we had won, and that everybody else on the team had played tougher and harder just to carry my load, like I was some kind of idiot. I'd walk out of that meeting room and I'd be so [ticked]—I mean, so [ticked]—I would have punched a hole in the wall.

And I wouldn't want to talk to anybody, eat anything, nothing. I'd spend the rest of the day by myself, just sittin' in my room, and I'd think about it and think about it and think about it, and by the next day, I couldn't wait to hit somebody.

And that's what he wanted to do, I knew that's what he was doin', and he still did it to me. Every damn time.

—*Randy White*

Tom Landry at his NFL Hall of Fame induction in August 1990.
(AP/Wide World Photos)

11

Landry and Leadership

~

 HOW COULD a guy who never screamed at anyone lead anyone? Landry showed the way. His players knew how he lived a pure life, a disciplined life with a work ethic that matched his family ethic.

Year in and year out, as he failed to waver from his habits, that example *was* his leadership.

Maybe he didn't give a lot of deep, sage advice to players, other than mentioning the Bible now and then. He led men by making them prepared—really, really prepared—to meet the Redskins or their Maker.

Tom Landry's special talent was in bringing out the best in others—which is the highest achievement any leader can attain.

—*Gerald Ford*

Whatever Tom told us to do was right. . . . A lot of times when we overrode that recommendation we got ourselves into trouble and we heard about it in the weekly film session.

—*Chuck Howley*

Every year in training camp, it wasn't like it is now. With him, veterans had to earn their places. Veterans like Lilly or Jordan stayed on their toes. There was always a fear of who would get cut or traded. You don't see that now.

—*Walt Garrison*

His work ethic was rigid. His study ethic was rigid, because we would be tested each week. He didn't lead by yelling. He led by example. His idea was that if you were well prepared, you didn't need a pep talk and it wasn't his nature to give them. I think he was really just a shy person. He led us by example, making us one of the best-prepared teams in the NFL.

—*Bob Lilly*

It wasn't an accident that Dallas was so successful. The Cowboys had a plan and the chief architect of that plan was Tom Landry. This guy could have been just about anything he wanted to be because he had a ferocious will to win and brains leaking out his ears.

They throw the word *genius* around pretty loosely these days, but that's what Landry is. Most of us are copiers. And if you're a really smart guy, you figure out what the best things are and why they're the best and you use them. You copy.

Landry's a couple light-years ahead of that. He's the kind of guy who invents the stuff the rest of us copy.

—*Walt Garrison*

He'd teach us to set goals, then achieve them, then set
a high set of goals and achieve them, until we did
things we didn't know we could do.

—*Chuck Howley*

Patience was one of the things he had a lot of and
something when I was younger I didn't have a lot of.
But I've gotten more over the years. As time has gone
on, I have more patience with myself, my kids my
family. That all goes back to Coach Landry. I have
never known a more patient person, and I guess it
came through probably because of his faith.

—*Walt Garrison*

We were in our twenties, so sure, we got mad at him,
but we always respected him. He was a weird person to
figure out, but he was a genius and mainly he was just
an introvert.

—*Lee Roy Jordan*

THE FIRST REQUIREMENT OF LEADERSHIP IS KNOWLEDGE. WHEN I BECAME PLAYER-COACH OF THE NEW YORK GIANTS' DEFENSE IN 1954, I WAS ONLY TWENTY-NINE YEARS OLD. I COULD NOT ESTABLISH MY AUTHORITY BASED ON AGE OR EXPERIENCE; I WAS YOUNGER AND HAD LESS EXPERIENCE THAN SEVERAL MEMBERS OF THE DEFENSIVE TEAM I COACHED. AND I WASN'T THE MOST TALENTED DEFENSIVE PLAYER ON THE TEAM; OTHERS HAD MORE ATHLETIC TALENT AND FOOTBALL SKILL. WHAT I DID HAVE IS KNOWLEDGE.[1]

—*Landry.*

Tom led by example and I tried to emulate him. It made me a different person.

—*Chuck Howley*

A LEADER DOESN'T HAVE TO BE THE SMARTEST MEMBER OF A GROUP, BUT HE DOES HAVE TO DEMONSTRATE A MASTERY OF HIS FIELD. MASTERY MEANS MORE THAN JUST KNOWING INFORMATION AND FACTS; IT REQUIRES AN UNDERSTANDING OF THE INFORMATION AND THE ABILITY TO APPLY THAT INFORMATION.[2]

—Landry

He was able to teach us what he meant. I can remember lots of times one of the assistant coaches would start explaining some new deal, some wrinkle on what we had been doing because that's what they decided was going to work for the next opponent, and we're all sitting around blinking and staring and not understanding.

Then Landry would come in, look at the problem, talk to us for five minutes—in that dry monotone that never changed—and do five more minutes on the blackboard, and we had it, man. It was there, clear and easy to understand. It was a gift, you know? He was a very gifted teacher, because being a coach is really just being a teacher, when you come down to it. You're just teaching grown men.

—Drew Pearson

IF I HAD TO PICK MY GREATEST STRENGTH AS A PRO-
FESSIONAL FOOTBALL COACH, I'D SAY IT WAS INNOVA-
TION. BUT IT STARTED WITH PREPARATION AND
KNOWLEDGE. AS A LEADER, YOU HAVE TO UNDERSTAND
THE PRESENT SYSTEM, SITUATION, OR PROBLEM YOU'RE
FACED WITH BEFORE YOU CAN REACT EFFECTIVELY—
BEFORE YOU CAN BE A SUCCESSFUL INNOVATOR. I HAD
TO UNDERSTAND THE INTENTIONS OF THE CLEVELAND
BROWNS' OFFENSE BEFORE I COULD DESIGN A COORDI-
NATED 4-3 DEFENSE TO COUNTER IT . . . A SUCCESSFUL
LEADER HAS TO BE INNOVATIVE. IF YOU'RE NOT ONE
STEP AHEAD OF THE CROWD, YOU'LL SOON BE A STEP
BEHIND EVERYONE ELSE.[3]

—Landry

He looked at football the way it was being played at the time and he devised completely new systems on offense and defense to beat that game. And for the last twenty years, the rest of the league has been trying to understand and then copy what Landry invented. That's called a genius.

—*Walt Garrison*

Tom is a person who stays in control under great stress of fire. He could handle any kind of job. He's just one of those unique people. If he were running the country or the state as governor, a lot of problems would be solved. But he also would make a fine president of Delta Air Lines. He has a tremendous understanding of so many things.[4]

—*Gil Brandt, former Cowboys personnel director*

Endnotes

Landry and His Youth

1. Tom Landry with Gregg Lewis, *An Autobiography: Tom Landry*. New York: Zondervan Books, 1990, 41
2. Ibid., 42
3. Bob St. John, *The Landry Legend: Grace Under Pressure*. Dallas: Word, 1989, 82.
4. Landry and Lewis, 46.
5. Ibid., 47
6. Ibid., 49-50.
7. St. John, 82.
8. Landry and Lewis, 50–51.
9. Ibid., 51
10. Skip Bayless, *God's Coach*. New York: Simon and Schuster, 1990, 112–13.
11. St. John, 115.

Landry and Humor

1. Landry and Lewis, 180.
2. Ibid., 211.
3. St. John, 57.
4. Landry and Lewis, 223.

5. Dave Klein *Tom and the 'Boys*. New York: Zebra Books, 1990, 195–96.
6. Ibid., 180–81.

Landry and Family
1. Landry and Lewis, 79.
2. Ibid., 86.
3. Ibid., 88.
4. Ibid., 200.
5. St. John, 143.
6. Ibid., 303.

Landry and His Men
1. Klein, 174.
2. Ibid., 179.
3. St. John, 2.
4. Klein, 157.
5. St. John, 140.
6. Ibid., 67.
7. Landry and Lewis, 196.
8. St. John, 149.
9. Klein, 133.
10. Ibid., 134.
11. Ibid., 158.
12. Ibid., 180–81.
13. Ibid., 159.
14. Bayless, 49.

Landry and Faith
1. Bayless, 19.
2. Ibid., 49–50.
3. Landry and Lewis, 120.
4. Ibid., 145–146.
5. Landry and Lewis, 148.
6. St. John, 154.
7. Ibid., 9.
8. Bayless, 52.
9. Ibid., 57–58.
10. Ibid., 86–87.

Landry and Football
1. Landry and Lewis, 87.
2. St. John, 133.
3. Ibid., 55–56.
4. Ibid., 16
5. St. John, 279.
6. Bayless, 91.
7. Landry and Lewis, 209.
8. St. John, 3.
9. Landry and Lewis, 246.
10. Ibid., 255–56.

Landry and Fashion
1. Landry and Lewis, 219–20.
2. Bayless, 100.

Landry and "the Face"
1. Klein.
2. St. John, 9.
3. Landry and Lewis, 145.
4. Ibid., 145.
5. St. John, 16

Landry and Motivation
1. Landry and Lewis, 276.
2. Ibid., 269.

Landry and Leadership
1. Landry and Lewis, 277.
2. Ibid. 278.
3. Ibid., 280–81.
4. St. John, 3.

Other Reviewed Material
Garrison, Walt, with John Tullius, *Once a Cowboy*. New York:
     Random House, 1988.
Guideposts magazine
Dallas Morning News
Dallas Times Herald

Acknowledgments

To the home typing staff: Joe Kaski, Jan McDaniel, and Ethan McDaniel. Also thanks for the advice and counsel of Skip Bayless, author of *God's Coach,* and to the former Dallas Cowboys kind enough to lend their time for this book.